Love So...

WILLIAM SHAKESPEARE

A Phoenix Paperback

The Sonnets by William Shakespeare first published
by J. M. Dent in 1976

This abridged edition published in 1996 by Phoenix
a division of Orion Books Ltd
Orion House, 5 Upper St Martin's Lane, London WC2H 9EA

Cover illustration: *L'Amour et Psyché*
by Francois Eduoard Picot © Réunion des Musées Nationaux

ISBN 1 85799 575 9

Typeset by CentraCet Ltd, Cambridge
Printed in Great Britain by
Clays Ltd, St Ives plc

Contents

O, *how much more doth beauty beauteous seem* 19
Not marble nor the gilded monuments 20
Being your slave, what should I do but tend 21
Like as the waves make towards the pebbled shore, 22
Is it thy will thy image should keep open 23
Against my love shall be as I am now, 24
Since brass, nor stone, nor earth, nor boundless sea, 25
That thou are blam'd shall not be thy defect, 26
No longer mourn for me when I am dead 27
That time of year thou mayst in me behold 28
But be contented when that fell arrest 29
So oft have I invok'd thee for my Muse 30
Whilst I alone did call upon thy aid, 31
O, how I faint when I of you do write, 32
I grant thou wert not married to my Muse 33
I never saw that you did painting need, 34
Farewell, thou art too dear for my possessing, 35
When thou shalt be dispos'd to set me light 36
Some glory in their birth, some in their skill, 37
So shall I live supposing thou art true, 38
Some say thy fault is youth, some wantonness, 39
From you have I been absent in the spring 40
My love is strengthen'd, though more weak in
   seeming. 41

To me, fair friend, you never can be old;   42

Let not my love be call'd idolatry,   43

When in the chronicle of wasted time   44

O never say that I was false of heart,   45

Let me not to the marriage of true minds   46

That you were once unkind befriends me now,   47

O thou my lovely boy, who in thy power   48

In the old age black was not counted fair,   49

My mistress' eyes are nothing like the sun;   50

Thou art as tyrannous, so as thou art,   51

So, now I have confess'd that he is thine,   52

When my love swears that she is made of truth,   53

O, call not me to justify the wrong   54

In faith, I do not love thee with mine eyes,   55

Two loves I have, of comfort and despair,   56

My love is as a fever, longing still   57

O me, what eyes hath Love put in my head,   58

Who will believe my verse in time to come,
If it were fill'd with your most high deserts?
– Though yet, heaven knows, it is but as a tomb
Which hides your life, and shows not half your parts.
If I could write the beauty of your eyes
And in fresh numbers number all your graces,
The age to come would say 'This poet lies;
Such heavenly touches ne'er touch'd earthly faces.'
So should my papers, yellow'd with their age,
Be scorn'd, like old men of less truth than tongue,
And your true rights be term'd a poet's rage
And stretched metre of an antique song.
  But were some child of yours alive that time,
  You should live twice: in it, and in my rhyme.

Shall I compare thee to a summer's day?
Thou art more lovely and more temperate.
Rough winds do shake the darling buds of May,
And summer's lease hath all too short a date;
Sometime too hot the eye of heaven shines,
And often is his gold complexion dimm'd,
And every fair from fair sometime declines,
By chance or nature's changing course untrimm'd;
But thy eternal summer shall not fade
Nor lose possession of that fair thou ow'st,
Nor shall death brag thou wander'st in his shade,
When in eternal lines to time thou grow'st.
    So long as men can breathe or eyes can see,
    So long lives this, and this gives life to thee.

20

A woman's face with Nature's own hand painted
Hast thou, the master-mistress of my passion;
A woman's gentle heart, but not acquainted
With shifting change as is false women's fashion;
An eye more bright than theirs, less false in rolling,
Gilding the object whereupon it gazeth;
A man in hue, all hues in his controlling,
Which steals men's eyes and women's souls amazeth.
And for a woman wert thou first created,
Till Nature as she wrought thee fell a-doting,
And by addition me of thee defeated
By adding one thing to my purpose nothing.
    But since she prick'd thee out for women's pleasure,
    Mine be thy love, and thy love's use their treasure.

So is it not with me as with that Muse
Stirr'd by a painted beauty to his verse,
Who heaven itself for ornament doth use,
And every fair with his fair doth rehearse,
Making a couplement of proud compare
With sun and moon, with earth and sea's rich gems,
With April's first-born flowers, and all things rare
That heaven's air in this huge rondure hems.
O let me, true in love, but truly write,
And then believe me, my love is as fair
As any mother's child, though not so bright
As those gold candles fix'd in heaven's air.
    Let them say more that like of hearsay well;
    I will not praise, that purpose not to sell.

My glass shall not persuade me I am old
So long as youth and thou are of one date;
But when in thee time's furrows I behold,
Then look I death my days should expiate.
For all that beauty that doth cover thee
Is but the seemly raiment of my heart,
Which in thy breast doth live, as thine in me;
How can I then be elder than thou art?
O therefore, love, be of thyself so wary
As I, not for myself, but for thee will,
Bearing thy heart, which I will keep so chary
As tender nurse her babe from faring ill.

    Presume not on thy heart when mine is slain:
    Thou gav'st me thine not to give back again.

Let those who are in favour with their stars
Of public honour and proud titles boast,
Whilst I, whom fortune of such triumph bars,
Unlook'd-for joy in that I honour most.
Great princes' favourites their fair leaves spread
But as the marigold at the sun's eye,
And in themselves their pride lies buried,
For at a frown they in their glory die.
The painful warrior famoused for might,
After a thousand victories once foil'd
Is from the book of honour razed quite,
And all the rest forgot for which he toil'd.
    Then happy I, that love and am belov'd
    Where I may not remove nor be remov'd.

When, in disgrace with Fortune and men's eyes,
I all alone beweep my outcast state,
And trouble deaf heaven with my bootless cries,
And look upon myself and curse my fate,
Wishing me like to one more rich in hope,
Featur'd like him, like him with friends possess'd,
Desiring this man's art and that man's scope,
With what I most enjoy contented least:
Yet in these thoughts myself almost despising,
Haply I think on thee, and then my state,
Like to the lark at break of day arising,
From sullen earth sings hymns at heaven's gate;
    For thy sweet love remember'd such wealth brings
    That then I scorn to change my state with kings.

When to the sessions of sweet silent thought
I summon up remembrance of things past,
I sigh the lack of many a thing I sought,
And with old woes new wail my dear time's waste.
Then can I drown an eye, unus'd to flow,
For precious friends hid in death's dateless night,
And weep afresh love's long since cancell'd woe,
And moan th'expense of many a vanish'd sight.
Then can I grieve at grievances foregone,
And heavily from woe to woe tell o'er
The sad account of fore-bemoaned moan,
Which I new pay as if not paid before.
      But if the while I think on thee, dear friend,
      All losses are restor'd, and sorrows end.

Thy bosom is endeared with all hearts
Which I by lacking have supposed dead;
And there reigns love, and all love's loving parts,
And all those friends which I thought buried.
How many a holy and obsequious tear
Hath dear religious love stol'n from mine eye
As interest of the dead, which now appear
But things remov'd that hidden in thee lie!
Thou art the grave where buried love doth live,
Hung with the trophies of my lovers gone,
Who all their parts of me to thee did give:
That due of many now is thine alone.
    Their images I loved I view in thee,
    And thou, all they, hast all the all of me.

35

No more be griev'd at that which thou hast done:
Roses have thorns, and silver fountains mud,
Clouds and eclipses stain both moon and sun,
And loathsome canker lives in sweetest bud.
All men make faults, and even I in this,
Authorizing thy trespass with compare,
Myself corrupting, salving thy amiss,
Excusing thy sins more than thy sins are;
For to thy sensual fault I bring in sense –
Thy adverse party is thy advocate –
And 'gainst myself a lawful plea commence,
Such civil war is in my love and hate,
    That I an accessory needs must be
    To that sweet thief which sourly robs from me.

Let me confess that we two must be twain,
Although our undivided loves are one;
So shall those blots that do with me remain,
Without thy help by me be borne alone.
In our two loves there is but one respect,
Though in our lives a separable spite,
Which, though it alter not love's sole effect,
Yet doth it steal sweet hours from love's delight.
I may not evermore acknowledge thee,
Lest my bewailed guilt should do thee shame,
Nor thou with public kindness honour me
Unless thou take that honour from thy name.
    But do not so. I love thee in such sort
    As, thou being mine, mine is thy good report.

38

How can my Muse want subject to invent
While thou dost breathe, that pour'st into my verse
Thine own sweet argument, too excellent
For every vulgar paper to rehearse?
O, give thyself the thanks, if aught in me
Worthy perusal stand against thy sight;
For who's so dumb that cannot write to thee,
When thou thyself dost give invention light?
Be thou the tenth Muse, ten times more in worth
Than those old nine which rhymers invoke,
And he that calls on thee, let him bring forth
Eternal numbers to outlive long date.

    If my slight Muse do please these curious days,
    The pain be mine, but thine shall be the praise.

Those pretty wrongs that liberty commits,
When I am sometime absent from thy heart,
Thy beauty and thy years full well befits,
For still temptation follows where thou art.
Gentle thou art, and therefore to be won,
Beauteous thou art, therefore to be assail'd;
And when a woman woos, what woman's son
Will sourly leave her till she have prevail'd?
Ay me! but yet thou mightst my seat forbear,
And chide thy beauty and thy straying youth,
Who lead thee in their riot even there
Where thou art forc'd to break a two-fold troth:
    Hers, by thy beauty tempting her to thee,
    Thine, by thy beauty being false to me.

That thou hast her, it is not all my grief,
And yet it may be said I lov'd her dearly;
That she hath thee is of my wailing chief,
A loss in love that touches me more nearly.
Loving offenders, thus I will excuse ye:
Thou dost love her because thou know'st I love her,
And for my sake even so doth she abuse me,
Suff'ring my friend for my sake to approve her.
If I lose thee, my loss is my love's gain,
And losing her, my friend hath found that loss:
Both find each other, and I lose both twain,
And both for my sake lay on me this cross.
    But here's the joy: my friend and I are one.
    Sweet flattery! Then she loves but me alone.

When most I wink, then do mine eyes best see,
For all the day they view things unrespected;
But when I sleep, in dreams they look on thee,
And, darkly bright, are bright in dark directed.
Then thou, whose shadow shadows doth make bright,
How would thy shadow's form form happy show
To the clear day with thy much clearer light,
When to unseeing eyes thy shade shines so!
How would, I say, mine eyes be blessed made
By looking on thee in the living day,
When in dead night thy fair imperfect shade
Through heavy sleep on sightless eyes doth stay!
    All days are nights to see till I see thee,
    And nights bright days when dreams do show thee me.

47

Betwixt mine eye and heart a league is took,
And each doth good turns now unto the other.
When that mine eye is famish'd for a look,
Or heart in love with sighs himself doth smother,
With my love's picture then my eye doth feast,
And to the painted banquet bids my heart;
Another time mine eye is my heart's guest
And in his thoughts of love doth share a part.
So either by thy picture or my love,
Thyself away are present still with me;
For thou not farther than my thoughts canst move,
And I am still with them, and they with thee;
    Or if they sleep, thy picture in my sight
    Awakes my heart to heart's and eye's delight.

48

How careful was I when I took my way
Each trifle under truest bars to thrust,
That to my use it might unused stay
From hands of falsehood, in sure wards of trust!
But thou, to whom my jewels trifles are,
Most worthy comfort, now my greatest grief,
Thou best of dearest and mine only care,
Art left the prey of every vulgar thief.
Thee have I not lock'd up in any chest
Save where thou art not, though I feel thou art –
Within the gentle closure of my breast,
From whence at pleasure thou mayst come and part;
    And even thence thou wilt be stol'n, I fear,
    For truth proves thievish for a prize so dear.

So am I as the rich, whose blessed key
Can bring him to his sweet up-locked treasure,
The which he will not ev'ry hour survey,
For blunting the fine point of seldom pleasure.
Therefore are feasts so solemn and so rare,
Since, seldom coming, in the long year set,
Like stones of worth they thinly placed are,
Or captain jewels in the carcanet.
So is the time that keeps you as my chest,
Or as the wardrobe which the robe doth hide,
To make some special instant special blest
By new unfolding his imprison'd pride.
    Blessed are you whose worthiness gives scope,
    Being had, to triumph, being lack'd, to hope.

54

O, how much more doth beauty beauteous seem
By that sweet ornament which truth doth give!
The rose looks fair, but fairer we it deem
For that sweet odour which doth in it live.
The canker blooms have full as deep a dye
As the perfum'd tincture of the roses –
Hang on such thorns, and play as wantonly
When summer's breath their masked buds discloses;
But for their virtue only is their show
They live unwoo'd and unrespected fade –
Die to themselves. Sweet roses do not so;
Of their sweet deaths are sweetest odours made:
    And so of you, beauteous and lovely youth,
    When that shall vade, by verse distils your truth.

55

Not marble nor the gilded monuments
Of princes shall outlive this powerful rhyme,
But you shall shine more bright in these contents
Than unswept stone besmear'd with sluttish time.
When wasteful war shall statues overturn
And broils root out the work of masonry,
Nor Mars his sword nor war's quick fire shall burn
The living record of your memory.
'Gainst death and all oblivious enmity
Shall you pace forth; your praise shall still find room
Even in the eyes of all posterity
That wear this world out to the ending doom.
    So, till the judgement that yourself arise,
    You live in this, and dwell in lovers' eyes.

57

Being your slave, what should I do but tend
Upon the hours and times of your desire?
I have no precious time at all to spend,
Nor services to do, till you require.
Nor dare I chide the world-without-end hour
Whilst I, my sovereign, watch the clock for you,
Nor think the bitterness of absence sour
When you have bid your servant once adieu;
Nor dare I question with my jealous thought
Where you may be, or your affairs suppose,
But, like a sad slave, stay and think of naught
Save, where you are, how happy you make those.
    So true a fool is love that in your will,
    Though you do anything, he thinks no ill.

Like as the waves make towards the pebbled shore,
So do our minutes hasten to their end;
Each changing place with that which goes before,
In sequent toil all forwards do contend.
Nativity, once in the main of light,
Crawls to maturity, wherewith being crown'd
Crooked eclipses 'gainst his glory fight,
And Time that gave doth now his gift confound.
Time doth transfix the flourish set on youth
And delves the parallels in beauty's brow,
Feeds on the rarities of nature's truth,
And nothing stands but for his scythe to mow.
  And yet to times in hope my verse shall stand,
  Praising thy worth despite his cruel hand.

Is it thy will thy image should keep open
My heavy eyelids to the weary night?
Dost thou desire my slumbers should be broken,
While shadows like to thee do mock my sight?
Is it thy spirit that thou send'st from thee
So far from home into my deeds to pry,
To find out shames and idle hours in me,
The scope and tenor of thy jealousy?
O, no, thy love, though much, is not so great;
It is my love that keeps mine eye awake,
Mine own true love that doth my rest defeat,
To play the watchman ever for thy sake.
    For thee watch I, whilst thou dost wake elsewhere,
    From me far off, with others all too near.

Against my love shall be as I am now,
With Time's injurious hand crush'd and o'erworn;
When hours have drain'd his blood and fill'd his brow
With lines and wrinkles; when his youthful morn
Hath travell'd on to age's steepy night,
And all those beauties whereof now he's king
Are vanishing, or vanish'd out of sight,
Stealing away the treasure of his spring:
For such a time do I now fortify
Against confounding age's cruel knife,
That he shall never cut from memory
My sweet love's beauty, though my lover's life.
    His beauty shall in these black lines be seen,
    And they shall live, and he in them still green.

Since brass, nor stone, nor earth, nor boundless sea,
But sad mortality o'ersways their power,
How with this rage shall beauty hold a plea,
Whose action is no stronger than a flower?
O, how shall summer's honey breath hold out
Against the wrackful siege of batt'ring days
When rocks impregnable are not so stout,
Nor gates of steel so strong, but Time decays?
O fearful meditation! Where, alack,
Shall Time's best jewel from Time's chest lie hid,
Or what strong hand can hold his swift foot back,
Or who his spoil of beauty can forbid?
    O, none, unless this miracle have might,
    That in black ink my love may still shine bright.

That thou are blam'd shall not be thy defect,
For slander's mark was ever yet the fair;
The ornament of beauty is suspect,
A crow that flies in heaven's sweetest air.
So thou be good, slander doth but approve
Thy worth the greater, being woo'd of time;
For canker vice the sweetest buds doth love,
And thou present'st a pure unstained prime.
Thou hast pass'd by the ambush of young days
Either not assail'd, or victor being charg'd;
Yet this thy praise cannot be so thy praise
To tie up envy, evermore enlarg'd.
  If some suspect of ill mask'd not thy show,
  Then thou alone kingdoms of hearts shouldst owe.

No longer mourn for me when I am dead
Than you shall hear the surly sullen bell
Give warning to the world that I am fled
From this vile world, with vilest worms to dwell.
Nay, if you read this line, remember not
The hand that writ it; for I love you so
That I in your sweet thoughts would be forgot
If thinking on me then should make you woe.
O, if, I say, you look upon this verse
When I perhaps compounded am with clay,
Do not so much as my poor name rehearse,
But let your love even with my life decay,
    Lest the wise world should look into your moan,
    And mock you with me after I am gone.

That time of year thou mayst in me behold
When yellow leaves, or none, or few, do hang
Upon those boughs which shake against the cold,
Bare ruin'd choirs where late the sweet birds sang.
In me thou seest the twilight of such day
As after sunset fadeth in the west;
Which by and by black night doth take away,
Death's second self, that seals up all in rest.
In me thou seest the glowing of such fire
That on the ashes of his youth doth lie,
As the death-bed whereon it must expire,
Consum'd with that which it was nourish'd by.
> This thou perceiv'st, which makes thy love more
> strong,
> To love that well which thou must leave ere long.

But be contented when that fell arrest
Without all bail shall carry me away.
My life hath in this line some interest,
Which for memorial still with thee shall stay.
When thou reviewest this, thou dost review
The very part was consecrate to thee.
The earth can have but earth, which is his due;
My spirit is thine, the better part of me.
So then thou hast but lost the dregs of life,
The prey of worms, my body being dead,
The coward conquest of a wretch's knife,
Too base of thee to be remembered.
    The worth of that is that which it contains,
    And that is this, and this with thee remains.

So oft have I invok'd thee for my Muse
And found such fair assistance in my verse
As every alien pen hath got my use,
And under thee their poesy disperse.
Thine eyes, that taught the dumb on high to sing
And heavy ignorance aloft to fly,
Have added feathers to the learned's wing
And given grace a double majesty.
Yet be most proud of that which I compile,
Whose influence is thine and born of thee.
In others' works thou dost but mend the style,
And arts with thy sweet graces graced be;
  But thou art all my art, and dost advance
  As high as learning my rude ignorance.

Whilst I alone did call upon thy aid,
My verse alone had all thy gentle grace;
But now my gracious numbers are decay'd,
And my sick Muse doth give another place.
I grant, sweet love, thy lovely argument
Deserves the travail of a worthier pen,
Yet what of thee thy poet doth invent
He robs thee of, and pays it thee again.
He lends thee virtue, and he stole that word
From thy behaviour; beauty doth he give,
And found it in thy cheek: he can afford
No praise to thee but what in thee doth live.
    Then thank him not for that which he doth say,
    Since what he owes thee thou thyself dost pay.

80

O, how I faint when I of you do write,
Knowing a better spirit doth use your name,
And in the praise thereof spends all his might
To make me tongue-tied speaking of your fame!
But since your worth, wide as the ocean is,
The humble as the proudest sail doth bear,
My saucy bark, inferior far to his,
On your broad main doth wilfully appear.
Your shallowest help will hold me up afloat,
Whilst he upon your soundless deep doth ride;
Or, being wreck'd, I am a worthless boat,
He of tall building and of goodly pride.
    Then if he thrive and I be cast away,
    The worst was this: my love was my decay.

82

I grant thou wert not married to my Muse,
And therefore mayst without attaint o'erlook
The dedicated words which writers use
Of their fair subject, blessing every book.
Thou art as fair in knowledge as in hue,
Finding thy worth a limit past my praise;
And therefore art enforc'd to seek anew
Some fresher stamp of these time-bett'ring days.
And do so, love; yet when they have devis'd
What strained touches rhetoric can lend,
Thou, truly fair, wert truly sympathiz'd
In true plain words by thy true-telling friend;
    And their gross painting might be better us'd
    Where cheeks need blood: in thee it is abus'd.

83

I never saw that you did painting need,
And therefore to your fair no painting set;
I found, or thought I found, you did exceed
The barren tender of a poet's debt;
And therefore have I slept in your report,
That you yourself, being extant, well might show
How far a modern quill doth come too short,
Speaking of worth, what worth in you doth grow.
This silence for my sin you did impute,
Which shall be most my glory, being dumb;
For I impair not beauty, being mute,
When others would give life, and bring a tomb.
    There lives more life in one of your fair eyes
    Than both your poets can in praise devise.

Farewell, thou art too dear for my possessing,
And like enough thou know'st thy estimate.
The charter of thy worth gives thee releasing;
My bonds in thee are all determinate.
For how do I hold thee but by thy granting?
And for that riches where is my deserving?
The cause of this fair gift in me is wanting,
And so my patent back again is swerving.
Thyself thou gav'st, thy own worth then not knowing,
Or me to whom thou gav'st it else mistaking;
So thy great gift, upon misprision growing,
Comes home again, on better judgement making.
    Thus have I had thee as a dream doth flatter:
    In sleep a king, but waking no such matter.

88

When thou shalt be dispos'd to set me light
And place my merit in the eye of scorn,
Upon thy side against myself I'll fight,
And prove thee virtuous though thou art forsworn.
With mine own weakness being best acquainted,
Upon thy part I can set down a story
Of faults conceal'd, wherein I am attainted,
That thou in losing me shall win much glory,
And I by this will be a gainer too;
For bending all my loving thoughts on thee,
The injuries that to myself I do,
Doing thee vantage, double-vantage me.
    Such is my love, to thee I so belong,
    That for thy right myself will bear all wrong.

Some glory in their birth, some in their skill,
Some in their wealth, some in their body's force,
Some in their garments (though new-fangled ill),
Some in their hawks and hounds, some in their horse;
And every humour hath his adjunct pleasure,
Wherein it finds a joy above the rest.
But these particulars are not my measure;
All these I better in one general best.
Thy love is better than high birth to me,
Richer than wealth, prouder than garments' cost,
Of more delight than hawks or horses be;
And having thee of all men's pride I boast –
    Wretched in this alone, that thou mayst take
    All this away, and me most wretched make.

93

So shall I live supposing thou art true,
Like a deceived husband; so love's face
May still seem love to me, though alter'd new,
Thy looks with me, thy heart in other place.
For there can live no hatred in thine eye,
Therefore in that I cannot know thy change.
In many's looks the false heart's history
Is writ in moods and frowns and wrinkles strange,
But heaven in thy creation did decree
That in thy face sweet love should ever dwell;
Whate'er thy thoughts or thy heart's workings be,
Thy looks should nothing thence but sweetness tell.
    How like Eve's apple doth thy beauty grow,
    If thy sweet virtue answer not thy show!

96

Some say thy fault is youth, some wantonness,
Some say thy grace is youth and gentle sport.
Both grace and faults are lov'd of more and less;
Thou mak'st faults graces that to thee resort.
As on the finger of a throned queen
The basest jewel will be well esteem'd,
So are those errors that in thee are seen
To truths translated, and for true things deem'd.
How many lambs might the stern wolf betray
If like a lamb he could his looks translate!
How many gazers mightst thou lead away
If thou wouldst use the strength of all thy state!
    But do not so. I love thee in such sort
    As, thou being mine, mine is thy good report.

From you have I been absent in the spring
When proud pied April, dress'd in all his trim,
Hath put a spirit of youth in everything,
That heavy Saturn laugh'd and leapt with him.
Yet nor the lays of birds nor the sweet smell
Of different flowers in odour and in hue
Could make me any summer's story tell,
Or from their proud lap pluck them where they grew;
Nor did I wonder at the lily's white,
Nor praise the deep vermilion in the rose.
They were but sweet, but figures of delight
Drawn after you, you pattern of all those;
  Yet seem'd it winter still, and, you away,
  As with your shadow I with these did play.

My love is strengthen'd, though more weak in seeming.
I love not less, though less the show appear.
That love is merchandiz'd whose rich esteeming
The owner's tongue doth publish everywhere.
Our love was new and then but in the spring
When I was wont to greet it with my lays,
As Philomel in summer's front doth sing,
And stops her pipe in growth of riper days –
Not that the summer is less pleasant now
Than when her mournful hymns did hush the night,
But that wild music burdens every bough,
And sweets grown common lose their dear delight.

    Therefore like her I sometime hold my tongue,
    Because I would not dull you with my song.

To me, fair friend, you never can be old;
For as you were when first your eye I eyed,
Such seems your beauty still. Three winters cold
Have from the forests shook three summers' pride;
Three beauteous springs to yellow autumn turn'd
In process of the seasons have I seen,
Three April perfumes in three hot Junes burn'd
Since first I saw you fresh, which yet are green.
Ah yet doth beauty like a dial-hand
Steal from his figure, and no pace perceiv'd;
So your sweet hue, which methinks still doth stand,
Hath motion, and mine eye may be deceiv'd.
    For fear of which, hear this, thou age unbred:
    Ere you were born was beauty's summer dead.

Let not my love be call'd idolatry,
Nor my beloved as an idol show,
Since all alike my songs and praises be
To one, of one, still such, and ever so.
Kind is my love today, tomorrow kind,
Still constant in a wondrous excellence.
Therefore my verse, to constancy confin'd,
One thing expressing, leaves out difference.
'Fair, kind, and true' is all my argument,
'Fair, kind, and true' varying to other words,
And in this change is my invention spent,
Three themes in one, which wondrous scope affords.
    Fair, kind, and true have often liv'd alone,
     Which three till now never kept seat in one.

When in the chronicle of wasted time
I see descriptions of the fairest wights,
And beauty making beautiful old rhyme
In praise of ladies dead and lovely knights;
Then in the blazon of sweet beauty's best,
Of hand, of foot, of lip, of eye, of brow,
I see their antique pen would have express'd
Even such a beauty as you master now.
So all their praises are but prophecies
Of this our time, all you prefiguring,
And for they look'd but with divining eyes,
They had not skill enough your worth to sing;
    For we which now behold these present days
    Have eyes to wonder, but lack tongues to praise.

O never say that I was false of heart,
Though absence seem'd my flame to qualify.
As easy might I from myself depart
As from my soul, which in thy breast doth lie;
That is my home of love. If I have rang'd,
Like him that travels, I return again,
Just to the time, not with the time exchang'd,
So that myself bring water for my stain.
Never believe, though in my nature reign'd
All frailties that besiege all kinds of blood,
That it could so preposterously be stain'd
To leave for nothing all thy sum of good;
    For nothing this wide universe I call,
    Save thou, my rose; in it thou art my all.

Let me not to the marriage of true minds
Admit impediments. Love is not love
Which alters when it alteration finds,
Or bends with the remover to remove.
O no, it is an ever-fixed mark
That looks on tempests and is never shaken;
It is the star to every wand'ring bark,
Whose worth's unknown although his height be taken.
Love's not Time's fool, though rosy lips and cheeks
Within his bending sickle's compass come;
Love alters not with his brief hours and weeks,
But bears it out even to the edge of doom.
    If this be error and upon me prov'd,
    I never writ, nor no man ever lov'd.

That you were once unkind befriends me now,
And for that sorrow which I then did feel
Needs must I under my transgression bow,
Unless my nerves were brass or hammer'd steel.
For if you were by my unkindness shaken
As I by yours, y'have pass'd a hell of time,
And I, a tyrant, have no leisure taken
To weigh how once I suffer'd in your crime.
O that our night of woe might have remember'd
My deepest sense how hard true sorrow hits,
And soon to you, as you to me then, tender'd
The humble salve which wounded bosoms fits!
    But that your trespass now becomes a fee;
    Mine ransoms yours, and yours must ransom me.

O thou my lovely boy, who in thy power
Dost hold Time's fickle glass, his sickle hour,
Who hast by waning grown, and therein show'st
Thy lovers withering as thy sweet self grow'st –
If Nature, sovereign mistress over wrack,
As thou goest onwards still will pluck thee back,
She keeps thee to this purpose, that her skill
May Time disgrace, and wretched minutes kill.
Yet fear her, O thou minion of her pleasure!
She may detain but not still keep her treasure.
Her audit, though delay'd, answer'd must be,
And her quietus is to render thee.

In the old age black was not counted fair,
Or if it were, it bore not beauty's name;
But now is black beauty's successive heir,
And beauty slander'd with a bastard shame:
For since each hand hath put on nature's power,
Fairing the foul with art's false borrow'd face,
Sweet beauty hath no name, no holy bower,
But is profan'd, if not lives in disgrace.
Therefore my mistress' eyes are raven-black,
Her brow so suited, and they mourners seem
At such who, not born fair, no beauty lack,
Sland'ring creation with a false esteem.
    Yet so they mourn, becoming of their woe,
    That every tongue says beauty should look so.

My mistress' eyes are nothing like the sun;
Coral is far more red than her lips' red.
If snow be white, why then her breasts are dun;
If hairs be wires, black wires grow on her head.
I have seen roses damask'd, red and white,
But no such roses see I in her cheeks;
And in some perfumes is there more delight
Than in the breath that from my mistress reeks.
I love to hear her speak, yet well I know
That music hath a far more pleasing sound.
I grant I never saw a goddess go:
My mistress when she walks treads on the ground.
    And yet, by heaven, I think my love as rare
    As any she belied with false compare.

Thou art as tyrannous, so as thou art,
As those whose beauties proudly make them cruel,
For well thou know'st to my dear doting heart
Thou art the fairest and most precious jewel.
Yet, in good faith, some say that thee behold,
Thy face hath not the power to make love groan.
To say they err I dare not be so bold,
Although I swear it to myself alone.
And, to be sure that is not false I swear,
A thousand groans, but thinking on thy face,
One on another's neck, do witness bear
Thy black is fairest in my judgement's place.
    In nothing art thou black save in thy deeds,
    And thence this slander, as I think, proceeds.

So, now I have confess'd that he is thine,
And I myself am mortgag'd to thy will,
Myself I'll forfeit, so that other mine
Thou wilt restore to be my comfort still.
But thou wilt not, nor he will not be free,
For thou art covetous, and he is kind.
He learn'd but surety-like to write for me
Under that bond that him as fast doth bind.
The statute of thy beauty thou wilt take,
Thou usurer that put'st forth all to use,
And sue a friend came debtor for my sake;
So him I lose through my unkind abuse.
  Him have I lost; thou hast both him and me;
  He pays the whole, and yet am I not free.

138

When my love swears that she is made of truth,
I do believe her, though I know she lies,
That she might think me some untutor'd youth
Unlearned in the world's false subtleties.
Thus vainly thinking that she thinks me young,
Although she knows my days are past the best,
Simply I credit her false-speaking tongue;
On both sides thus is simple truth suppress'd.
But wherefore says she not she is unjust?
And wherefore say not I that I am old?
O, love's best habit is in seeming trust,
And age in love loves not to have years told.
　　　Therefore I lie with her, and she with me,
　　　And in our faults by lies we flatter'd be.

O, call not me to justify the wrong
That thy unkindness lays upon my heart;
Wound me not with thine eye but with thy tongue;
Use power with power, and slay me not by art.
Tell me thou lov'st elsewhere, but in my sight,
Dear heart, forbear to glance thine eye aside:
What need'st thou wound with cunning when thy might
Is more than my o'erpress'd defence can bide?
Let me excuse thee: 'Ah, my love well knows
Her pretty looks have been mine enemies,
And therefore from my face she turns my foes,
That they elsewhere might dart their injuries.'
    Yet do not so; but since I am near slain,
    Kill me outright with looks, and rid my pain.

In faith, I do not love thee with mine eyes,
For they in thee a thousand errors note;
But 'tis my heart that loves what they despise,
Who in despite of view is pleas'd to dote.
Nor are mine ears with thy tongue's tune delighted,
Nor tender feeling to base touches prone;
Nor taste nor smell desire to be invited
To any sensual feast with thee alone;
But my five wits nor my five senses can
Dissuade one foolish heart from serving thee,
Who leaves unsway'd the likeness of a man,
Thy proud heart's slave and vassal-wretch to be.
 Only my plague thus far I count my gain,
  That she that makes me sin awards me pain.

144

Two loves I have, of comfort and despair,
Which like two spirits do suggest me still.
The better angel is a man right fair,
The worser spirit a woman colour'd ill.
To win me soon to hell my female evil
Tempteth my better angel from my side,
And would corrupt my saint to be a devil,
Wooing his purity with her foul pride.
And whether that my angel be turn'd fiend
Suspect I may, yet not directly tell;
But being both from me, both to each friend,
I guess one angel in another's hell.
      Yet this shall I ne'er know, but live in doubt
      Till my bad angel fire my good one out.

147

My love is as a fever, longing still
For that which longer nurseth the disease,
Feeding on that which doth preserve the ill,
Th'uncertain sickly appetite to please.
My reason, the physician to my love,
Angry that his prescriptions are not kept,
Hath left me, and I desperate now approve
Desire is death, which physic did except.
Past cure I am, now reason is past care,
And frantic mad with evermore unrest.
My thoughts and my discourse as madmen's are,
At random from the truth, vainly express'd;
    For I have sworn thee fair, and thought thee bright,
    Who art as black as hell, as dark as night.

O me, what eyes hath Love put in my head,
Which have no correspondence with true sight!
Or if they have, where is my judgement fled,
That censures falsely what they see aright?
If that be fair whereon my false eyes dote,
What means the world to say it is not so?
If it be not, then Love doth well denote
Love's eye is not so true as all men's 'no'.
How can it, O, how can Love's eye be true,
That is so vex'd with watching and with tears?
No marvel then, though I mistake my view:
The sun itself sees not till heaven clears.
     O cunning Love, with tears thou keep'st me blind,
     Lest eyes, well seeing, thy foul faults should find.